MW00897891

Dreaming

30 days of dreaming with God

Dreaming

30 days of dreaming with God

SIMCHA NATAN

simchanatan.com

fb.com/simchanatan
IG: Simcha Natan

Dreaming *30 days of dreaming with God* © Simcha Natan 2018

Cover illustration by Joe Hately © Simcha Natan

Design and layout © HerebyDesign

Edited by Abbie Robson

The right of Name to be identified as the author of
this work has been asserted by her/him in accordance with the
Copyright, Designs and Patents Act 1988.

All rights reserved. Without limiting the rights under copyright reserved
above, no part of this publication may be reproduced, stored in or
introduced into a retrieval system, or transmitted, in any form or by any
means (electronic, mechanical, photocopying, recording or otherwise),
without the prior written permission of the above publisher of this book.

Unless otherwise indicated, all Scripture quotations are taken from the
Holy Bible, New International Version Anglicised Copyright © 1979,
1984, 2011 Biblica. Used by permission of Hodder & Stoughton Ltd, an
Hachette UK company. All rights reserved.
or
New King James Version (NKJV)
Scripture taken from the New King James Version®. Copyright © 1982
by Thomas Nelson. Used by permission. All rights reserved.

For Izak

*The dreams that God has put in your heart
are bigger than you know.*

*He has the best adventure planned for you, and I pray for
courage for you to daily dream with God.*

I'm your biggest fan x

Contents

Contents

DREAMING WITH GOD

Introduction

This devotional is intended to take you on a journey of discovery, not only of the dreams which you may have in your heart, but also of what God may be doing in your life right now to prepare you for the fulfillment of those dreams, or even to reveal new dreams that he may have for you.

It may confront dreams you thought were dead, or resurrect childhood dreams, or it may give you new ones. The hope is that you will find fresh release to dream with God the way he longs and always intended to dream with you.

The content of this booklet is inspired by Simcha's book *Dare to Ask* about dreaming with God, as a foundation on which this devotional is built.

DAY 1

Dreaming with God

*"He has made everything beautiful in its time.
Also he has put eternity in their hearts, except that
no one can find out the work that God does from
beginning to end."*
Ecclesiastes 3:11

God is a God of dreams. He loves us to imagine, create, and think outside of our own little bubbles, because that is where he is found, and he longs for us to join him. God isn't locked into a linear time line, with all the rules and constructs that we have created. He created us with an imagination that can perceive things differently from the reality we're in, able to dream things and hope for things that are 'other'. These things are not always founded on our daily life and routine, they can transcend it, taking us far beyond what is naturally possible.

We are not designed to live life aiming for the end date of our physical death. God has put eternity in our hearts, and our dreams, deep passions and yearnings come from a place that echoes with eternity. This world can sometimes corrupt us with selfish desire and worldly wisdom, but God can always restore us to a place where we can sit with him and think bigger.

DREAMING WITH GOD

We can't grasp what God is doing across time, and we don't know how our story affects those around us. We don't know if the things we imagine and dream will ever come to pass. But what we do know is that he has made us to spend an eternity with him. He has promised to make everything beautiful in its time. If only we would trust our time into his hands.

The more we connect our deepest dreaming and hoping with his, the more we will hear his heartbeat. We will start to notice that some of the dreams we thought were a part of our identity were actually hollow, and they'll fall away. The passions we're left with are the ones that God placed there from the foundations of the earth, those that will resound throughout eternity.

Make a conscious effort today to dream with God. Whether you're standing at the kitchen sink dreaming about being on a stage, working as a waitress dreaming about studying at university, or feeding a screaming baby dreaming about sleep, join with God in those thoughts and passions, asking him to truly reveal which of those dreams are from him and which are not connected to his eternal purpose.

DAY 2

In me all things are possible

*"My God sent his angel, and he shut the mouths of the
lions. They have not hurt me"*
Daniel 6:22

Daniel was put into a den of lions that were most likely kept
hungry for the very purpose of killing those who disobeyed
the king. He was preserved from a situation that seemed
pretty impossible. But God…

I don't know if you have ever walked through a painful or
difficult season in life, where you feel nothing but anguish
in your soul – I know that I have. And the thing that has
remained constant in all those seasons is that no matter how
bad the situation got, I was always eventually able to say "But
God…"

We are so quick to restrict God's abilities in our world, because
we like to put human boundaries on him and what he can do.
But he has proven over and over again that those boundaries
do not apply to him. He rescued the Israelites from slavery
and fed them with manna in the desert, he walked on water,
he raised the dead, and he knows your every thought.

Our dreams might seem enormous; they may be 'other

worldly' in comparison to where we're at today. They might feel so far away that we don't know how we're ever going to get there. But God...

Yesterday you joined with God, connecting your dreams with his eternal purposes. You invited him to speak into your private hopes and aspirations, the things that we don't ever share with other humans. Very few people actually think these dreams will ever come to pass, because we are trained by this world to think very little of ourselves. We need to constantly remind ourselves of God's opinion of us, not the world's.

In Genesis 3:8, we read that Adam and Eve heard God walking in the garden in the cool of the day. God had come to take a stroll with the crown of his creation. Life looks a little different now. We don't hear or see God, so we have to trust that he is walking with us all day. He didn't give up, he made a way for us to dwell with him every day. To talk with him, dream with him, rest with him.

And if he can do that, he can do anything.

For what do you need more faith to believe God can do?

DAY 3

A new thing

"Behold, I am doing a new thing;
now it springs forth, do you not perceive it?"
Isaiah 43:19

I love how God has to check that Isaiah and his listeners noticed that he is doing a new thing! "Do you not perceive it?" - "hello? Can you not tell?"

God is always doing a new thing because he is a creator. It is part of who he is, to create where there was nothing before. The word used in Genesis to describe creation is not a word that refers to making something out of something else. He didn't create the universe like we would create a pot out of clay. He made it where there was nothing before. He is a master craftsman. He is always doing something new.

What we really need to do in this situation is to ask "what new thing is he doing in me?"

There is no time in our lives when God hasn't been at work. It may not have felt like it, it may not have looked like it, and it may have taken a long time for us to comply with the new thing that God was working on. But he is always doing a new thing - we just take a while to catch on!

A NEW THING

Yesterday we read about how all things are possible with God. So is it not true that God can take a person who believes they're through, over the hill, forgotten or invisible, and do a new thing? God never stops believing in us and his perfect plan for our lives, and he is constantly working to bring us through every situation, so that they can be used for good, to achieve his purposes in and through our lives, for the sake of his glory.

You see, even in the old things, God can do a new thing. Even in the old dreams of our youth, or the childhood aspirations we had, God can do a new thing.

Take some time today to ask God to give you the eyes to see the new thing he is doing in you. Ask him to take whatever it is that you're struggling with, and ask him to do a new thing.

DAY 4

All things made perfect

"But he said to me, "My grace is sufficient for you, for my power is made perfect in weakness." Therefore I will boast all the more gladly about my weaknesses, so that Christ's power may rest on me"
2 Corinthians 12:9

The amazing thing about God is that he knows we're weak. He knows we've done wrong. He knows every detail of our thought life and what is really in our hearts. And yet he still says in his word that 'his power is made perfect in our weakness".

Isn't that incredible? This is a truly loving God.

God wants us to believe that he has plans for us. Plans to prosper us in his perfect way and timing, plans to connect us with his eternal plan, to lavish gifts on us like a good father. However it might look externally, Romans 8:28 tells us that in all things he is working for our good. Yet how often do we foolishly believe that our weakness is greater than God's strength, and that in some way we can mess up his perfect plan?

All we really need is this. His grace is enough.

This truth in and of itself is liberating, because we don't have to strive - he's already done it! We just have to accept his grace. Once we do that, we can stop apologizing for our weakness and simply let God take that weakness and make it his opportunity to display his goodness and might in our lives.

When God is given permission to use a weak person, they are raised up to a position that they never would have dreamed.

Look at Moses, a man, a murderer, a stutterer, hiding away in the desert trying to figure out who he was. God used Moses' weakness to display his might to Egypt, and he became one of the greatest heroes of our faith. He was still a man. He probably still stuttered, but God raised him up to a position that Moses would never have dreamed of having. That is not to say that Moses never made any more mistakes. But God never gave up on him. And God never gives up on us.

Take some time today to acknowledge your weaknesses, and invite God into them. Give them over to God, and expect him to use them as a platform for displaying his hand. Boasting in our weaknesses goes against everything within us, but remember, that's how Christ's power rests on us.

DAY 5

Eternity in our hearts

"Those who seek the Lord will praise him—may your hearts live forever!"
Psalm 22:26

We weren't designed just to live a mortal life and then be done and finished. We were designed to live on forever with our maker. What he has placed in us isn't just about our destiny here on earth, it is connected to God's eternal purposes.

This is a great comfort, because while we should be making the most of our God given life, we can rest assured that the essence of who we are here on earth will continue. Those things which God has placed in our hearts, the dreams, passions and gifts he has given us, will continue to outwork for all of eternity.

There is a tension in wrestling to get all that God has for us in this life and striving to be like him in all our ways, while still maintaining the peace of mind and the understanding that we have all of eternity to work out what he has put in our hearts.

Carrying eternity in our hearts is an indication that we are made in God's image (Ecc 3:11). When Yeshua ascended into heaven, he did not stop being all that he was on earth. He continues to be who he is, today. I'm not talking about him being the son of God, I'm talking about his personality, his character. When we meet him and are made like him (1 Thess 4:17) we will be made perfect, but that doesn't mean we will stop being who we are, it means that who we are will be perfected.

Sometimes we get a taste of eternity on earth when we are given the opportunity to start walking out who we are made to be. But sometimes we don't. There is a part of us that will only be fully active and fruitful when it is made perfect by him, in eternity.

Think about the things that you carry in your heart that maybe you have mourned not coming to pass, and take some time today to readjust how you view these things. This earthly life is only temporary, you're not done yet, and God has made you who you are for eternity, not just for this lifetime.

DAY 6

The road to Egypt

*"His brothers said to him, "Do you intend to reign
over us? Will you actually rule us?"
And they hated him all the more because of his dream
and what he had said"
Genesis 37:8*

In reading through Genesis, it would be natural to think of Egypt as an oppressive place, home to the Pharaoh who wouldn't let God's people go. We imagine a land of slavery and cruelty from which the Israelites had to be rescued.

In Joseph's story, though, God used Egypt in a very different way.

Joseph was a slave before he ever reached Egypt. His brothers were the ones who were cruel, and Egypt became his destination rather than the place of his captivity.

Egypt wasn't easy for Joseph; he was hidden away, falsely accused, imprisoned, seemingly on a roller coaster of promotions and disappointments. And yet it was in Egypt that God fulfilled the dreams he had shown Joseph all those years before, using his past experiences to make him ready for the dreams he'd had as a child. He made Joseph the man he needed to be to fulfill the plan that ultimately enabled the survival of the Israelites.

Sometimes we can look at the things we're walking through in our lives as horrible tangents from our interpretation of the dreams we have been given. Yet God knows exactly what we need to walk through to become who he has made us to be. He knows what will make us ready for our dreams. He gave us these dreams, and he wants to see them come to pass in a way that serves far beyond ourselves to his Kingdom purposes.

I'm sure Joseph questioned these childhood dreams when he was sitting in prison. He may have even laughed off the very notion of anyone, let alone his brothers, bowing down to him while he stood accused of adultery. But through every moment and trial, God was teaching him something while preparing him for what was to come.

Take some time today to think about some of the things which you may have walked through, that you may have viewed as tangents, or 'wrong turns' and ask God to show you what he was been teaching you in them.

DAY 7

Incubation and rest

"The Lord will fight for you; you need only to be still."
Ex 14:14

$\mathcal{I}$ think we all know what it feels like to push and force our way through when we want something. Persistence and the ability to persevere despite our circumstances are noble characteristics, ones that God often asks of us.

But even in our persistence, God wants us to be at rest. Instead of forcing and striving in situations that seem impossible, he will sometimes allow us to reach a dead end, where it feels as though nothing can be done to push things through.

When we step back to do things God's way, it may sometimes lead us to a season of incubation for our dreams. Incubation is by no means the same as inactivity. Incubating something means tending to something gently to help it grow. Disrupting the process will threaten its survival. Without incubation, an egg simply will not hatch.

Incubation and rest are a wonderful combination. Being forced to rest can be uncomfortable because we are action-orientated creatures. Yet there are things that still take time to incubate. With all of our technological advances, we have not managed to produce the instant baby!

24

Incubation and rest

The plans that God has given us need tending in the secret and quiet place. We are ever living in tension of resting and doing. God asks us to push into him for more, while sitting and waiting, wrestling while remaining at peace.

When the Israelites were standing on the edge of the Red Sea, afraid of the Egyptians who were closing in on them, Moses' response is simple:

> "Do not be afraid. Stand firm and you will see
> the deliverance the Lord will bring you today. The
> Egyptians you see today you will never see again.
> The Lord will fight for you; you need only to be
> still." (Ex 14: 13-14)

It is my repeated testimony that when I have had the grace to 'let go' of the details and let him take over, the end result and mission completed has always been far greater than I could have done on my own. If we do it our way, it's a human endeavor, which naturally produces human outcomes. When we allow ourselves to join in with God's endeavors, there is no limit to what he can do.

Take some time today to decide that you will be content to be still. Commit the things in your life and your heart to him, that you may be trying to fix or push through in your own strength. Meditate on the words from these verses, that God will deliver you. You need only be still.

Decide to make peace with the possibility that you may need to incubate something for a season before it comes to fruition.

DAY 8

Delight in the Lord

"Take delight in the LORD, and he will give you the
desires of your heart."
Psalm 37:4

Have you ever stopped to think about what it means to have God delight in you?

He didn't just create you and leave you to live your life without him - he delights in you! He knows every thought you have, each longing of your heart, the deep passions and desires you carry, and he delights in it all!

When we delight in someone, we ache to make them happy. We want them to have everything they desire and we go out of way to help that happen.

God is no different - in fact, I believe we possess this trait because we're made in his image, and this is how he views us. He may know more about the timing and motives that we have, and be able to control the circumstances for our best, but he does want to give us the desires of our hearts. He put them there! But most of all, he wants us to delight in him, in the same way that he delights in us.

The great thing about delighting in him is that the more we do it, the more we become like him. The more we become like him, the more the desires of our heart are tested and refined. This is a perfect exchange because as we begin to learn what our hearts really desire, the more those desires come to fruition, because they come from him. This is what John means by 'asking according to his will'.

> *This is the confidence we have in approaching*
> *God: that if we ask anything according to his will,*
> *he hears us. And if we know that he hears us—*
> *whatever we ask—we know that we have what*
> *we asked of him. (1 John 5:14-15)*

The time you have set aside to spend with God makes his heart full. That's what delight is, when the people you love the most love you back and there is a mutual investment in each other. It fills your heart and creates a place of love and trust.

Take some time today to think about what it is that you carry in your heart. Make a commitment to delight in him and to ask him for his desires for you. Often we find it difficult to believe that God would delight in us - ask him to reveal this to you, and delight in it!

DAY 9

In the quiet

"After the earthquake came a fire, but the LORD was not in the fire.
And after the fire came a gentle whisper."
1 Kings 19:12

Where do you best hear God?

I think we all kid ourselves that we hear God best in the worship nights, the conferences, the music, maybe even in a book. We find ways to get a spiritual high, which we can then attribute to God. We get so used to having a roller coaster relationship with God that we begin to equate spiritual highs with him feeling close, and the lows with him feeling far away.

What God actually wants is some peace and quiet! That is not to say that he can't be found in all those other things – God is everywhere and can always be found. By his grace he chooses to speak through so many things, including our sometimes inept, man-made ideas! But in today's verse the scriptures are clear: although earthquakes and fire made more impression, more impact and more noise, God didn't choose to reveal himself there. He was found in a gentle whisper.

The thing about a whisper is that in order to hear it, you

have to intentionally listen, and you can't intentionally listen to someone with noise all around you. Noise can take many forms. It could be visual noise, it could be emotional noise, it could be family noise – it could even be church noise. Whatever the noise is, we have to make a way to find a quiet place where we can hear his whisper. We have to incline our ear towards him.

When we hear God's whisper, we understand more of who he is, and in response to that, we begin to realize who we truly are. It is in these moments and these realizations that we start to comprehend which of the dreams we have in our hearts are really aligned with his dreams for us, and which are just human, empty aspirations.

Make a conscious effort today to clear the noise out of your life, just for a half hour. Position yourself to listen to his whisper and see what he has to say to you today.

DAY 10

In the still

"Be still before the LORD and wait patiently for him;
do not fret when people succeed in their ways, when
they carry out their wicked schemes."
Psalm 37:7

There is a difference between quiet and stillness.

When I think of stillness, I always imagine those scenes in the movies where time is suspended, and everything stops moving. It's not just that there's no noise, but that there is also no movement.

For me, being still before the Lord means to stop the movement. I imagine my current life suspended, like those movie scenes, where you can really see everything that's going on, and every detail held like a statue. You can walk around inside the scene and truly see it all for what it is, even the dust in the air.

But as well as being still, the scriptures tell us to 'wait patiently'. This implies a lack of doing. Waiting involves *not* doing something we could be doing, or were doing. This is hard because we are so good at fretting! We panic that we'll miss the time, or that we won't be able to manufacture circumstances as well as we otherwise would. We worry that we might miss our chance, or that someone else will do it first or better. But God is always found in the stillness, and in the quiet. There is no fretting in God. There is only peace and perfect timing.

The combination of being still and waiting is a powerful one. Being truly still allows God to show us the reality of what's going on around us in perfect clarity; stopping our constant 'doing' and waiting on him then gives him the opportunity to show what our next action should be.

Make a conscious effort today to be still, and to really allow God to take you on a tour of your life, to see it for what it really is. Give him the space to highlight things to you that he may want you to stop, or move, or change. Be patient and let him guide you, and he will give you the go signs and stop signs, and show you what to do next.

DAY 11

Streams in the desert

"See, I am doing a new thing! Now it springs up;
do you not perceive it? I am making a way in the
wilderness and streams in the wasteland."
Isaiah 43:19

There is a recurring theme in the Bible about God doing a new thing. One of the first examples of this is the flood. God wanted to start again, to do a new thing. It wasn't that he had done it wrong the first time, but rather that man had been corrupted. God promised he wouldn't ever flood the earth again, but he didn't promise never to do another new thing. And thank him that he didn't!

Over the past couple of days we've looked at the places we find God - in the still, and in the quiet. But do we ever consider meeting him in the desert?

We know that the desert is a dry, arid, dangerous place of extremes and survival. Yet through the story of Hosea, we learn that he allures us there.

He leads us, guides us, woos us to come with him into this place, because this is where we can be left in no doubt of who has transformed us.

I can remember the first time I took some time out to meet God in the desert. I was sat on dry, hard, 'dead' ground, with two shrubs on either side of me, full of dancing, flitting butterflies. Ahead of me, I could see the mountains rising up imposingly, and behind me was the Dead Sea. In front of me was a worn and barely visible path.

In this spot God spoke to me in a way that I have not experienced before. In direct contrast to the feelings the Israelites must have felt during their 40-year walk, God showed me that he actually wants me to *stay* in the desert. There was life and transformation all around, but the desert place was for me. For now.

There I was, in my little spot, with the glorious mountains ahead of me – my eyes fixed on the high places, bitter waters behind me. I was surrounded by life. But I was still in the desert.

This left me utterly undone. It all made sense to me for the first time in my life. I found myself praying that God would keep me in the desert: *'God would you keep me in the wilderness, I want to stay in a place of desperation for you, I want to stay in a place where you are my lifeline and my All in all.'*

If he can bring streams in the wasteland, imagine what he can do when you're walking through Eden!

If you're walking through a desert season, take heart! He has brought you here to meet with you, to speak tenderly to you, and to do a new thing. Thank him for the season you're in, and position your heart to be ready for the new thing that is coming!

33

DAY 12

Make straight

"Lead me, LORD, in your righteousness because of my enemies-- make your way straight before me."
Psalm 5:8

It isn't a magic formula that God gives us, that he will make our paths straight and our lives easy. Many believers think that if they follow God life will be easier for them, but the context of this verse says otherwise. David is in the presence of his enemies, and he is asking for God's help and assurance. He is crying out to God to make his paths straight.

Often we don't see the path that we're on as being straight; it can seems to be a winding, mess of country roads that seem intent on wrecking us! But what if, when we look back over our lives, we see this beautiful tapestry of intervention from God, where he leads us to places where he wanted to show us his glory, or reveal the secrets of his heart to us?

Maybe the roads that we thought were the most winding actually end up being the best way? We are often so intent on walking our own way that we don't notice the mountains we are climbing in the process!

God isn't interested in giving us an easy life. He's interested in partnering with us, and transforming us into his likeness along the way. We should be praying for God to lead us, like David did, but without attaching conditions. We should follow wherever he leads, because he knows what is best for us. If we find ourselves in the middle of a rigorous workout on a mountain windy climb, then we should trust that this is exactly what we need.

Sometimes the straight path of the Lord can seem to be a messy path, by man's standards. David is definitely an example of a man doing 'foolish things' in the world's eyes. Yet he is one of the greatest examples of a worshiper, someone who walked with God. Some of his choices made no sense at all!

He gave up the opportunity to kill a murderous King Saul, sparing his life, knowing that with just one movement he could have ended his season of exile. He chose the path of honor, and refrained from the 'easy' path out of the desert.

And yet, through God's eyes, these were the straight paths, that have a direct route to the destination that God had for him. Indeed, this was the moment that Saul knew David would be king after him:

> *And now, behold, I know that you shall surely be king, and that the kingdom of Israel shall be established in your hand. 1 Sam 24:20*

Pray today that God would make clear his way for you, that he would give you peace in the knowledge that the paths you're taking are his straight ways, that lead exactly to where he wants you to go.

DAY 13

Move mountains

"I will go before you and will level the mountains; I will break down gates of bronze and cut through bars of iron."
Isaiah 45:2

Faith that moves mountains. I would love to see a mountain move! The thing I love about these verses is that they indicate the immensity of God's love for us. He is love, his essence is love, and if we cannot possess that love, then we are nothing. We are supposed to imitate Christ in all things, and he is love.

But this isn't a weak or basic love, the way you or I might love a TV program or a cup of tea. His love for us is fierce. He is passionately engaged with our stories, our lives and the details of our destinies, because he wants us to be passionately engaged with his story, and how we can work with him in his perfect plan. He will go to great lengths to enable his plan for our lives to take place. He will level mountains, he will break down gates, because he is committed to us.

Our dreams and passions are put there by God. He wants us to trust that he has a plan for those dreams and passions. Every passion has a purpose - to point to him and glorify him.

36

When we learn to love others like he loves, or at least catch a glimpse of what loving like that means, then he can truly partner with us. No matter what the mountain might look like, if we want to see it move, and we have the faith to see them move, first of all we must learn to love.

> "If I have the gift of prophecy and can fathom all mysteries and all knowledge, and if I have a faith that can move mountains, but do not have love, I am nothing." 1 Cor 13:2

Take some time today and ask God to reveal his heart of love to you. It may be the love he has for someone else that you get a glimpse of, or it may be the love he has for you. When we truly see love, and learn to love as he does, then our faith becomes something that is a force to be reckoned with, because our hearts are beating in time with his.

Day 14

For freedom

*"It is for freedom that Christ has set us free. Stand
firm, then, and do not let yourselves be burdened
again by a yoke of slavery."*
Galatians 5:1

I love the lack of agenda that there is in this verse.

God didn't set us free so that we could do X, Y or Z for him.
He set us free, so we could be free. We still have a choice
of what we do with that freedom. We can take the gift of
salvation, and live our lives according to all the benefits and
blessings that come with that, but miss the greatest gift of all.

When you are a slave, you have no choices. Your will is
irrelevant and you have no place to speak an opinion or share
a thought. You are a commodity. This is not what God intends
for our lives to be like.

When we are set free, we are free! We can go where we want
to go, do what we want to do and share any thoughts or
opinions we may have. Anything is possible! We have the
freedom to choose anything, but the real crux of God giving
us our freedom is so that we can choose him.

For freedom

These days we may not look like slaves on the outside, but we can so easily end up enslaved by less visible things, be that friendships, technology, food, pornography or any of a million other things that people find themselves in slavery to. But God gave us freedom. We can choose.

When Rahab was given her freedom after the fall of Jericho, in Joshua 6:25, she could have chosen to live any life she wanted. But with her freedom, Rahab chose to abide with God's chosen people.

In the same way, we are given freedom. God doesn't want a forced relationship, or a relationship that looks like that of a master and a slave. He wants us to choose him, as he has chosen us.

Today is all about choices. Make a fresh commitment today to choose God, to accept the freedom that he has offered you. Stand firm, knowing that you are no longer burdened by slavery, but free!

Day 15

Letting go of entitlement

*"I know that everything God does will endure
forever; nothing can be added to it and nothing taken
from it. God does it so that people will fear him."*
Ecclesiastes 3:14

Our dreams are not something we're entitled to. They are a part of who we're made to be, but, as we've already studied, we are eternal beings designed to live eternally with God.

This verse can be a great comfort to us, because what God does will endure forever. We can't undo his work or ruin his plans, because they were there before the foundation of the world and continue throughout eternity. We have all of eternity to realize who we are in him, and our dreams are a part of that. Both our dreams and the motives behind them will be made perfect in him, as will we.

Often we are intent on making our dreams and visions happen for ourselves. We push through and try to force God's hand. This is a dangerous place, because we start to trust ourselves rather than trusting in God.

When the Bible says nothing can be added to or taken away from God's plan, this means we can rest. We can't force our dreams to happen the way we want them to. We can trust that nothing can be added or taken away from God's plan for our life. God can move mountains (Is 45:2), part seas (Ex 10:19) and walk on water (Matt. 14:29), so we can rest assured that he is strong enough to fulfill what he has planned for us.

God promises an abundance of blessings to those who live a life laid down for him. The Bible tells us that it's the one who trusts in the Lord and whose confidence is in him that is blessed (Jer 17: 7). We don't have any entitlement to the blessings of God, including the fulfillment of our dreams. That's not how it works!

Take time today to search your heart and make sure that your assurance is found in him. It's so easy to hold on to entitlement, especially when dreams and visions are the subject matter. But the blessing lies in trusting in the Lord. Not in our own confidence and abilities, but putting our confidence him.

DAY 16

Nothing is wasted

"When they had all had enough to eat, he said to his disciples, "Gather the pieces that are left over. Let nothing be wasted."
John 6:12

This verse is so powerful. When reading the whole of the story of the feeding of the five thousand it's easy to pass over these words. I know that I am usually drawn to think only of the number of people who've eaten their fill and the leftover food that the disciples were asked to gather. But if we dig a little deeper into this verse, it reveals a principle that can transform how we view the events of our life.

Nothing is wasted.

In the last book of the Bible we read that we are headed to a marriage feast with the Lamb (Rev 19:9), presented as the pure and spotless bride made worthy of him. I don't believe that God will look back over our lives and say "those crumbs in his life - throw them away!" He takes all of the pieces, even the left over, spat out, moldy crumby parts of our life, and says, "let nothing be wasted." How liberating! He can use all things, and he can make all things new (Rev 21:5).

We often condemn ourselves to a life that is less than what God has planned for us because of past mistakes or poor choices. But God knows! He knew every choice we would make along the way and he will still not let our lives go to waste. If we give him control of the basket of bread that is our life, he will use it all. Not only the good parts, but also the very things that we think have ruined us. All the 'leftovers' can be redeemed and made to be the greatest tools when placed in his hands.

Nothing we do is a surprise to our maker. He has a habit of taking our greatest failures and making them his greatest opportunities - if we would only invite him in.

Have a think about what you would consider the 'crumbs' of your life to be. Decide to let God gather them and use them. He will not let anything be wasted if we give them to him.

DAY 17

Lift your hands

"When Moses' hands grew tired, they took a stone and put it under him and he sat on it. Aaron and Hur held his hands up--one on one side, one on the other--so that his hands remained steady till sunset."
Exodus 17:12

But he said to me, "My grace is sufficient for you, for my power is made perfect in weakness." Therefore I will boast all the more gladly about my weaknesses, so that Christ's power may rest on me. That is why, for Christ's sake, I delight in weaknesses, in insults, in hardships, in persecutions, in difficulties. For when I am weak, then I am strong.
2 Corinthians 12:9-11

Lifting our hands in worship in times of celebration and joy can be easy. It is natural to praise in the good times. But life isn't always easy. We grow tired or we feel like we just can't stand any longer, not just physically but emotionally and spiritually. Life does a really good job of wearing us down and draining us of energy.

So what about those times we are too tired to look up? What then?

Lift your hands

It is difficult to wrap our heads around the fact that it is when we are at our most tired and drained that we most need to lift our hands and look up. It is in doing this that we gain strength and are able to make the statement that we choose to turn to him for our strength and peace in our weakest moments. That is when we will know his supernatural strength giving us the ability to keep going, even when we feel we are at the end of ourselves.

When Moses held his arms up, the battle continued to be won. When he put his hands down, the battle started to be lost. It is the action of choosing to keep worshiping before him that gives us strength. This logic often goes against our natural instinct of wanting to curl up in a ball and hide from the world, but it is a Biblical principle that we see echoed throughout scripture. Sometimes God may lead us to a place where we are not surrounded by a community that can hold us up, yet we still have no option but to lift our hands.

Whatever season of life you're in, take some time today to choose to lift your hands. Whether you're in a time of overflowing joy or a time of drought and frailty, lift your hands to him and allow his strength to be your strength.

DAY 18

Practice what you preach

*"Now go; I will help you speak and will teach you
what to say."*
Exodus 4:12

We all have God given gifts. Some of them we might know about, some might be lying dormant, but they're there. Moses didn't know he possessed the gift of leadership; he had run away from responsibilities and leadership and hidden in the desert for 40 years, enjoying a quiet, peaceful life with the Midianites.

The burning bush experience was a rude interruption to his quiet life of tending to sheep and enjoying his wife! Despite what God was commanding, Moses still worried about his ability to carry out what was being asked of him. He questioned God's choice of him so much so that God had to say "enough"!

Moses didn't know the gifts or destiny that God had made him for, but God met him where he was, taking compassion on his insecurities, even indulging them with signs and miracles, and with the words to use.

The thing is, Moses had the ability to practice what God had asked of him all along. Once he knew what God had told him to say he could go over it and practice it. We can do the same thing. If God has asked us to do something, or put a gift in us for something, we can practice it, using it in the secret place until he puts us in the setting where it's required.

Maybe a gift of yours is obvious, but unused. Maybe God has spoken a new thing to you, but you haven't yet stepped out into it. Practice! Take the information that God has given you, and don't be afraid to ask for more. Moses dared to ask God for a lot of information that he didn't originally have, and God gave him what he needed. Don't be afraid to practice what God has asked you to do, to prepare yourself for when you're ready to go.

Take some time today and think about your dreams, your hopes, and your gifts. Maybe there is something you can start to invest time in that has laid dormant, and you can start to awaken the gift. Don't be afraid of putting time into it, even if you don't know what it's for yet.

Day 19

Blind obedience

"But Samuel replied: "Does the Lord delight in burnt offerings and sacrifices as much as in obeying the Lord? To obey is better than sacrifice, and to heed is better than the fat of rams."
1 Samuel 15:22

Blind obedience is hard for humans, because we're programed to need or want more information and we simply don't like trusting when we don't have it. And yet obedience is the best sacrifice we can make.

Often, it's the decision to obey that is harder than the obedience itself. Once we've made the decision to obey, the sacrifices that have to be made along the way seem less 'sacrificial', because we're obeying the voice of One who called, and there is no greater act.

We may not ever be done with this lesson, but we are always given opportunities for God to fully prove himself to us.

Trusting and obeying don't come naturally to most of us, so we often don't give God the chance to prove himself. Actually, God will always be faithful when he asks us do something. He will always hold up his end of the bargain, because it's in his character to be faithful - he cannot be anything else. It's actually us who are the problem in this test we put before God. We wait for God to do his bit before we are willing to do our bit. But that's not how it works.

How can we know he'll hold us up, if we never step out of the boat?
How can we know he'll open the door, if we never approach it?
How can we know he'll bring things to life, if we never let him breathe on it?
Actually, our test of God, is really a test of us.

God never changes. He's always faithful. He's always true. He will always surprise us. It's us who need to trust that our obedience will always be seen, always be rewarded one way or another, even if it's in ways we don't expect.

Today, decide to take the safety net away, and let him hold you up as you step out onto the waters. Decide to obey him without any conditions or deals and trust that he will come through on his end, because he is always faithful.

DAY 20

An audience of One

"Then your Father, who sees what is done in secret,
will reward you."
Matthew 6:6

"I will give you hidden treasures, riches stored in se-
cret places, so that you may know that I am the Lord,
the God of Israel, who summons you by name."
Isaiah 45:3

In Matthew 6, Yeshua mentions doing things in secret three times: fasting, praying and giving. If we are to be content with fasting, praying and giving in secret, why stop there? We can also be content with being a secret worshiper, or a dancer, or a painter... There is no end to what you could insert here!

The world is consumed with making everyone our audience, through pictures, fashion, music and video. Everyone has Facebook, Twitter, Instagram, Snapchat or a blog of some sort! We are brainwashed into thinking that the world needs to know what we had for breakfast! So of course it is now harder to be content when we don't have an audience for the things we are called to or are gifted in.

The point is that if we aren't content with him being our only audience, then we aren't ready for an audience at all.

This scripture has become incredibly counter-cultural. It is a foreign concept to lock ourselves away, hide away from the world, and pour our gifts out just for his delight, even if it means we never do it for any other audience.

Doing things in secret has become something that we have associated with negative or bad things, but doing something and deliberately keeping it from others isn't necessarily bad. Yeshua instructed us to pray in a way that kept others from knowing that we were praying, to fast in a way that wasn't obvious, and to give in a way that didn't advertise our generosity. Likewise, we should worship in a way that doesn't flaunt our talent and study in a way that doesn't intimidate.

During your day today, see if you can find a way to strategically lock yourself away for 10 minutes and invest into a gift that you haven't done before. Be intentional in your secrecy, and begin to train yourself to be content with knowing you have an audience of One.

DAY 21

Riches in Heaven

"Do not store up for yourselves treasures on earth,
where moths and vermin destroy, and where thieves
break in and steal.
But store up for yourselves treasures in heaven, where
moths and vermin do not destroy, and where thieves
do not break in and steal. For where your treasure is,
there your heart will be also."
Matthew 6:19-21

Following yesterday's study of the secret place, these verses about storing up treasure are a good progression. So how do we do it? What does it mean to store up treasures in heaven?

Again, it's counter-cultural to what we are bombarded with on a daily basis: bucket lists, the pressure to travel the world and do everything you can before you die, and "you only live once." But what if the whole point of life on earth is to prepare us for where we actually spend the vast majority of our time – eternity in heaven? What if everything we do here is preparation for life with him? Nothing we do here on earth is without consequence, it all has eternal significance.

Think back to the secret place we thought about yesterday, and picture it as an investment bank. Every time we invest time in it, an eternal, heavenly treasure pot grows. These are the investments that we will one day arrive to. They are the things that will not waste away or become null and void; they are the things that will bless God's heart and that he will reward us for.

What if the things that God put in your heart are not only for this life on earth, but also for the next life we have in him? I think God wants to us to have an eternal perspective on our destiny and our gifts; he wants us to be happy to invest in them now, even if we have to wait for the fulfillment to come in heaven.

Take some time today to think or journal honestly about where your riches are being stored. Sometimes we can find that we are storing up our treasure on earth without having noticed. Ask God if there is anything that needs to be adjusted or realigned to give us the right perspective again.

Day 22

The struggle

"But Jacob replied, "I will not let you go unless you bless me.""
Genesis 32:26

Even though the story of Jacob wrestling with God is one of my favorite examples of tenacity in the Bible, we will not focus on the fact that he wrestled with God today, but rather on the outcome of his struggle.

Jacob entered into this fight terrified to face up to his former sins, yet clinging onto God's promise of kindness.

> *"O Lord, you told me, 'Return to your own land and to your relatives.' And you promised me, 'I will treat you kindly." (Gen 32:9)*

Through his tenacity, Jacob was permanently marked by his encounter wrestling with the man who was God. He refused to let his relationship with Esau be defined by his sins and persisted in pushing through. He even dared to ask for a blessing, after which he was never the same again. Three remarkable things happened as a result of this battle. He was physically changed by this encounter, he received a new name, and he saw the face of God.

Jacob could have stopped when God told him to stop, but out of his desperation he kept pressing in. In his darkest moment, he refused to give up on God's kindness without pushing for more.

If we too push through into God for his blessing, we cannot remain the same. So what if we decided to not be satisfied with the status quo? What if we refused to let our mistakes define us or our future? What if we decided today to keep wrestling for God's blessing in the face of our greatest challenges, or for the things that we have been praying for?

We, too, can receive a new name or identity, and encounter the face of God. We are so often content to stop pressing in because we didn't get what we asked for first time. We stop wrestling because our circumstances tell us we're wrong to believe there's more. But what if the whole point is that when we press in and push through, everything changes?

Today is a day for a big prayer. Do you dare to ask God for more? To decide to wrestle and press in for more? Are you ready for an encounter with God, to see him face to face? Maybe it's time to lock arms with God and cling onto his kindness, not letting go until you receive the blessing. He will mark you so you're never the same again.

DAY 23

The fire

"If we are thrown into the blazing furnace, the God we serve is able to deliver us from it, and he will deliver us."
Daniel 4:17

We all go through seasons in life that feel like we're walking through fire. It's a scary place. It's suffocatingly hot, inescapable and lonely.

The thing that is striking about the story of Shadrach, Meshach and Abednego was that God didn't rescue them before they were thrown into the fire, he allowed them to be tossed into the furnace. Those who were fortunate enough to witness this miracle were amazed both by the fact that they emerged alive, and also by the lack of evidence from the hardship they'd been through.

We, too, are sometimes faced with hardships that are just like walking through the fire. This story marks a process that God also takes us through. He allows us to pass through seasons of fire that are necessary to purify and refine us.

The fire is also the place where God shows up. He doesn't leave us in the flames forever, they are only ever there as a refining season in our lives. But it is during those times of intensity that he shows up most vividly, as he did for the three men in the flames.

Shadrach, Meshach and Abednego trusted God completely and absolutely, and God knew what they could cope with. He knew their limits, and how much time in the flames would make the greatest impact on them, on the guards watching, on the King, and ultimately on the nation. Our seasons in the flames are not only about us and our refinement, they reach beyond us into the world around us, further than we could know.

Make a decision today to trust God with the season you're in. If it is already a season of flames, take comfort in the story of the three men in the fire. If you are not in a season of flames, we can always be sure that there will come a fiery season, so decide today to trust God, whatever you are walking through, knowing that it is all in preparation for something that is coming.

DAY 24

The war

"For our struggle is not against flesh and blood, but against the rulers, against the authorities, against the powers of this dark world and against the spiritual forces of evil in the heavenly realms."
Ephesians 6:12

We all struggle. The Bible never promises us an easy life or a problem free existence. We all have areas that seem to be dogged by insecurity, disbelief, or what appears to be plain bad luck. The Bible is clear that these struggles are not against people of flesh and blood, but against spiritual forces. Sometimes spiritual forces use circumstances and people around us to wage a war on us, but it is important to see the bigger picture in these attacks.

Our greatest areas of struggle are often an indication of our greatest gifting or calling. The war on our lives can be targeted, planned and strategic - so much so that we don't give the enemy enough credit. He is already defeated, and he knows that, but it doesn't stop him wreaking havoc during this period of time that he has the freedom to do so.

The enemy also uses the strategy of gradual wearing down to stop us from living to our potential and according to the destiny that God has for us. One of the greatest threats to the enemy is a believer who is so secure in their walk with God that they can see attack for what it is, and keep their eyes on the prize through it all.

> *"If God is for us, who can be against us?... No, in all these things we are more than conquerors through him who loved us." Romans 8:31-37*

The important thing is to not be afraid of the war. God can use the war to make us stronger, to refine our skills, to give us stickability and to strengthen us spiritually, physically and emotionally. But this is only possible if we see this spiritual crusade for what it is. It is a war! The minute we say "yes" to living a life for God we have to train and be equipped to deal with the battle that we are engaged in.

Ask God today to reveal to you the greatest areas of attack in your life and make a decision to be more aware of that which the enemy might be trying to destroy or corrupt. Pray that he will show you the strategies and spiritual weapons to fight the fight, and not be conquered.

Day 25

The strategy

"For the Spirit God gave us does not make us timid, but gives us power, love and self-discipline."
2 Timothy 1:7

"Finally, be strong in the Lord and in his mighty power. Put on the full armor of God, so that you can take your stand against the devil's schemes."
Ephesians 6:10-11

Our greatest strategy is to continually be purifying ourselves ready to live and work with a Holy God. It is His kindness that leads us to repentance, and from this place of humility and worship we can rise up in power and be clothed with strength.

He has given us all we need to stand firm and keep walking forwards in our purpose and calling. The fact that you have made it to day 25 of this study means that you are living daily in the Word, which is your greatest tool and weapon against the enemy and his attacks.

"No temptation has overtaken you except what is common to mankind. And God is faithful; he will not let you be tempted beyond what you can bear. But when you are tempted, he will also provide a

way out so that you can endure it." 1 Cor. 10:13

We cannot do what we do not hear or know from God. We can only do what is asked of us in God's Word. The strategy, really, is trust. If we do what God has told us to do, we can be strong in the Lord, put on his armor and stand firm, then we can trust that he will do the rest. Just as David trusted God when he approached Goliath, we can trust that all that we do will be like David's pebbles in the face of the enemy.

We so often like to sit down and concoct our own plans and strategies to manipulate our dreams into being, but when David picked up those smooth pebbles from the brook, I doubt he had 'becoming King' as the long game in his mind! He trusted God, he was faithful with what was in his hand, and God saw. God honored him, and God made him King.

Take the time today to 'put on' the armor of God like David did. He didn't wear physical armor, but he operated as a warrior of God and trusted that God would use his small offering of a pebble. God saw him and David's giant came tumbling down. If you have giants that you can identify in your life, take some time to clothe yourself in the armor God has given you, and be ready for God to use your small offerings to bring the giants down.

DAY 26

The victory

"I have told you these things, so that in me you may have peace. In this world you will have trouble. But take heart! I have overcome the world."

"Rise up; this matter is in your hands. We will support you, so take courage and do it."

John 16:33, Ezra 10:4

Many of us struggle in our everyday lives, but we can take heart – these are only a temporary difficulties. When we are feeling completely overwhelmed with life, we can rest in the assurance that he has already won this battle. We are on the winning team!

Because he has already overcome, we can live daily in victory, which simply means stepping out from under any cloud of guilt or condemnation. We so often just accept our situation, the same way we just expect the clouds in the sky. But God wants us to see that the sky is clear, there is no cloud - we can walk and run under an open heaven of blessing and release.

When it comes to our dreams and passions, the pains and scars from our past can often cripple us from being able to step out and take courage. We doubt we are covered, we doubt we are ready, and we doubt that we're able. But as Shekaniah says to Ezra in today's verse, "This matter is in your hands, take courage and DO IT!"

Obviously we must seek God's timing when we look to step out into something new, but so often God has open doors ready for us that we don't see because we are too busy looking at the clouds instead of seeing the clear sky. We set up camp outside the door, waiting for God to push us through, when actually, we just need to keep moving forwards, stepping through the open doorway into what God has for us.

Take today to release to God the clouds you may be living under, and to accept the clear skies available by his sacrifice. Pray that God would reveal his timing, show you the doors he has for you, give you the courage to step through into his plan.

DAY 27

Abundance

"You let people ride over our heads; we went through fire and water, but you brought us to a place of abundance."

"They feast on the abundance of your house; you give them drink from your river of delights."
Psalm 66:12, 36:8

We often don't believe that God wants us to live with an abundance. We have a poverty mindset and believe that 'having' is wrong. We think we should live by faith, not by seeking more 'stuff'.

But what if God isn't referring to material possessions? What if God wants us to have an abundance mindset that is not materialistic, but based on abundance in him?

God is the God of gifts. When he sent the Holy Spirit, he came with marvelous, inexplicable gifts. With his gifts come fruit and the fullness of all that he has for us, if we only accept that he wants to give abundantly.

The story of the Samaritan woman is a story of abundance. She didn't get it when Jesus told her that he would give her water - she thought in natural terms. She probably thought it a little strange that this man was offering her water while standing right next to a well full of the stuff! She didn't understand that he wanted to offer her an abundance of life, a life that she had never had and never thought she deserved.

Like her, we can have a tendency to think we're undeserving, yet we aren't. It is one of the deepest mysteries in our faith that the God of the universe would see us as deserving of his love and affection, let alone an abundance of it.

Earlier in this devotional plan we have looked at walking through the fire. Here we have a promise of what is waiting for us after we have walked through the fire - abundance! This goes against everything that should naturally happen after walking through a fire. There should be less, not more! But with God, things don't follow the natural rules.

Once you have walked through a fire, you have been refined. Today, bring to mind all the chaff that has been burned up and begin to walk into the abundance God has for you, precious and pure.

DAY 28

Rest

*"Truly my soul finds rest in God;
my salvation comes from him.*

*Truly he is my rock and my salvation;
he is my fortress, I will never be shaken."*
Psalm 62: 1-2

There is a paraphrase of Daniel 3:18 that I love. In the face of being thrown into the fire, Daniel assures the king that God will save them, "and even if not, he is still good."

This is a beautiful expression of a heart at rest. If we truly believe that God is still good "even if not", then we can rest and have peace in anything that comes our way. One of the enemy's greatest ploys is to tempt us to doubt the goodness of God and his intentions towards us. The moment that we doubt this we are thrown into unrest, turmoil and doubt. It unravels all that our belief system in God is based on. If God isn't good, then it calls into question everything.

It is of vital importance that we question regularly if our soul truly finds rest in God. We often assume that's the case, but I have found that I need to truly search my heart and mind to check that I am believing in the goodness of God. Often when I feel down, unsettled or frustrated, I find that I've somehow doubted his goodness, and I've questioned if the situation I'm in is of him, or his hand is truly on it. But if I believe that God is good, and his hand is upon me, then "I will never be shaken".

Doubt, turmoil, depression and an unsettled spirit are things that shake us at the very core. The verse for today says that when we find rest in God, we will never be shaken. There will always be times when we have to deal with very real questions and issues that come up in our walk, but we should always come at it with an intentional lens that God is always good. He cannot be anything else. It is the essence of who he is. In this fact, we can rest.

Take time today to change the lens through which you look at your life, or specific situations within your live, and decide to view those things from the perspective that GOD IS GOOD. Find the rest that is there for you, and take refuge in that fortress of rest that can never be shaken.

Day 29

Own it!

"For we are God's handiwork, created in Christ Jesus to do good works, which God prepared in advance for us to do."
Ephesians 2:10

Have you ever noticed how much time we spend fighting the season we're in? We start apologizing for our struggles, wallowing in self-pity, and going to great lengths to cheer ourselves up.

What if we decided to embrace where we're at, and to trust that God put us there for a reason, knowing that if we trust him we can find joy in any season? What if we stopped apologizing for the rough time we're having, and started being honest with ourselves and those around us, just saying "I'm struggling, but God is good"? What if we stopped feeling ashamed about the difficulties we're facing, as if it's an indication of how in control we are or how 'good' a person we are, and held our heads high knowing that if God is asking me to face this, he has something good to do, because he is good?

Sometimes we just have to own the seasons we're in without letting it get tainted by fake and unrealistic standards of normality. Everyone goes through seasons of hardship, struggles, depression, anger, disappointment and isolation. It's how we respond to these seasons that determines how long they will last. If we live in denial and put on the polite "I'm fine" mask, God has to break the mask down to get us to be real. If we own the season, and approach it with honesty, expectation and humility, it will pass by faster, and we will learn and receive more from God than we ever expected.

It is during these difficult seasons that the desires and dreams in our hearts feel most far away, and most impossible. And yet they are often just on the other side. That is half the test - to choose to believe that God is good; to choose to believe that it's not an accident that you're walking through this season. He has not given up on the potential in us - he's trying to bring it out.

Decide today to approach life from this new perspective. Every disappointment that comes your way, or moment of self-pity, or anxiety, turn it into an opportunity to own it. Say to yourself, "God has something for me to learn in this moment, he's not done with me yet." Hold your head high and embrace his goodness.

DAY 30

Dare to dream

*"His master replied, 'Well done, good and faithful
servant! You have been faithful with a few things;
I will put you in charge of many things. Come and
share your master's happiness!'"
Matt 25:23*

We have spent the past 30 days walking through a journey
of dreaming with God. It's never as simple as sitting down
and day dreaming about what great things we could achieve.
It's always about God preparing us for something so much
bigger and beyond us that he needs to lead us through the
preparation for it. And it never just ends with us, it is rather
for his Kingdom, his purposes and his glory.

The scripture for today is the story of the servants who were
all trusted with talents from their master, and what they all
did with it. You could replace the word 'talents' with dreams
to see the impact this story might have on us now.

It's not just about having dreams and visions for our lives,
it's about how we nurture and foster those dreams. How we
invest in the private times determines the level of partnership
we are seeking with God in these dreams. Like the servants
with the talents, it's up to us how we invest these passions,

dreams and visions. If we bury them, nothing will come of them. But if we have invested into them in the secret place we can see God multiply them before our eyes.

When your dreams and visions seem so far away that they seem impossible, don't lose heart! God doesn't give up on us. There isn't any step you've taken that he hasn't known about or had a plan for - even the ones which we thought had messed everything up. He saw it, he was there with you, and he can use it for good.

Maybe you've given up on your dreams and visions completely, and you've decided that you'll never amount to anything. Remember though, God raises life from the dead, and he can do it too with those parts of your heart that feel like they've just curled up and died. But it takes you, daring to dream again. Daring to create, daring to ask, daring to risk.

Maybe this devotional has caused you to remember things you used to dream about when you were younger or given you new dreams. Take some time to journal these, dedicate them to God and go back to day 1!

Reviews of Dare to Ask

What you are about to read is like a good movie with various characters, vantage points and visceral moments that are all connected by a common theme – one of great risk and great reward. I think there is something in all of us that wants to believe for great things. *Dare to Ask*, explores that belief by reintroducing a cast of biblical characters whose experiences and decisions clearly correlate with life's challenges and circumstances today.

Like a master archaeologist, Simcha skillfully brushes away the dust and debris that has covered over dormant dreams so that divine destiny can be rediscovered once again – not just the destination, but the process. The revelation in the title chapter alone is well worth the price of admission, but the waves of wisdom, insight, honesty and personal application continue to roll until the very last page.

Dare to Ask challenges the resigned mindset that we are merely silent spectators in this life and beautifully reminds us that dreams are possible, miracles are real and hope is attainable if you just dare to ask.

Steve Carpenter
Founder, Highway 19 Ministries – Jerusalem

~

To the reader of *Dare to Ask*, I would say that when you reach the end of the book, you will conclude that this has been a kairos moment. It is a serendipity, a surprise discovery. Instead of it focusing on aspects of worship from a gifted worship leader, you will be taken on a moving personal journey that deepens your love for the Messiah. It leaves a lot of questions unanswered, but you are left with the deep assurance that the Lord is in control. As readers, we are simply left to keep on asking and keep on trusting. This is a beautiful devotional book written from the heart.

Dr David Elms
International Christian Embassy Jerusalem UK Director

~

Dare To Ask has a beautiful tapestry of practicality and spirituality woven throughout the pages. It challenges readers to dream our God-given dreams, use our God-given gifts, and remove clutter from our hearts so that we can experience the fullness of what God has for us. Through her testimony and scriptural insights, Simcha demonstrates how to be grateful in all things – including trials and desert places. If you need encouragement, restoration or a fresh stirring of hope in your heart, you will find it here! Prepare to go deeper...

Michael & Sara Thorsby
Burn 24-7 New Bern, NC Directors (USA)

Available Now
simchanatan.com

OUT NOW

SIMCHA NATAN

simchanatan.com/dreaming-ep

22309567R00049

Made in the USA
San Bernardino, CA
14 January 2019